Boise State University Western Writers Series   Number 155

Frank Chin

By John Charles Goshert
Utah Valley State College

Editor: Tara Penry
Editorial Assistant: Cece Gadda
Cover Photo by Corky Lee,
Courtesy of Coffee House Press

Copyright 2002

Boise State University, Boise, Idaho

Copyright 2002
by the
Boise State University Western Writers Series

ALL RIGHTS RESERVED

Library of Congress Cataloging-in-Publication Data

Goshert, John Charles.
　Frank Chin / by John Charles Goshert.
　　p. cm. — (Boise State University western writers series ; no. 155)
　Includes bibliographical references.
　ISBN 0-88430-155-9 (alk. paper)
　1. Chin, Frank, 1940- 2. Authors, American—20th century—Biography.
3. Chinese Americans—California—Biography. 4. Asian American authors—Biography. 5. Chinese Americans in literature. 6. California—Biography. I. Title. II. Series.

PS3553.H4897 Z68 2002
813'.54--dc21

2002014092

Printed in the United States of America by
Boise State University Printing and Graphic Services
Boise, Idaho

Frank Chin

Frank Chin

FRANK CHIN AND THE WEST

Born in Berkeley in 1940, Frank Chin lived in the Motherlode country of California's Sierra foothills during the Second World War before returning to the San Francisco Bay Area. He attended the University of California at Berkeley as an English major, but was drawn away to work for railroad companies throughout the west. Such early experiences of movement and transience would provide the foundations for the shifting settings of much of his drama, fiction, and criticism that would follow; additionally, this transience would also underlie the complex tone, treatment, and perception of Asian American identity that characterizes his work and distinguishes Chin from many of his contemporaries in literature and criticism. As Dorothy Ritsuko McDonald comments, Chin has constantly worked to reclaim the history of Chinese Americans as a "valiant, vital part of the history of the American West," to counter dominant narratives and historical fantasies about passive, obedient, humble, and effeminate Asian Americans (ix). As though countering such preconceptions about Asian American passivity through physical as well as creative activity, Chin has led a relatively transient life, although primarily along Interstate 5 between Washington and California. "Fed up with the Bay Area," he recalls, Chin moved south to work with the East-West Players; and, although no longer with the group, he continues to live and work in Los Angeles.

When dealing with his own origins, as well as those of his literary characters and various nonfiction personae, Chin employs a longstanding racial epithet as his point of departure. He argues provocatively that the "Chinaman" arrives in America—and comes to claim a complicated space in American national consciousness—not from China, but rather from the American west. From his earliest works, Chin's characters find themselves negotiating origins and genealogies that disrupt not only their own senses of identity, but also longstanding American and European conceits about the polar opposition that firmly divides China from the "West." Tam Lum, the protagonist of Chin's first play, *The Chickencoop Chinaman* (1972), is found at the end of the play listening for ghosts of his great grandparents' generation to return to San Francisco from the railroad and mining camps on the Iron Moonhunter, an immigrant-made, mytho-historic train constructed of parts stolen from the railroad industry. As an originary space, then, Chin exposes California as an unstable place and idea; indeed, as we have come to learn through increasing attention to western American writing, the American west is a space infinitely capable of taking on meanings that are diffuse, contentious, and often conflicting. Compellingly, Chin takes on that complex history of identification and definition throughout his work, embracing the multiplicities not only of Chinese American identity, but also of American identity as a whole.

Activated by transience, shuttling between urban and rural spaces, the Sierras and the Bay Area, Seattle and Los Angeles, Chin decenters the geographic stability—indeed, the veritable demand for domesticity—that has historically been the prerequisite for Asian American writing. As Chin has suggested throughout his creative and critical work, the domestication of Asian America—whether geographically in Chinatown, or ideologically in passivity—has been a fundamental component of a broader project of

American racism; thus, in the face of the call to domestication, Chin has historically pursued a mobility of location—and, more importantly, a mobility of identity itself. Furthermore, he imagines multiple generations and cultural inheritances in tension; they do not cohere or coalesce into an identifiable concept of Chinese American identity or history, but rather into a complex hybrid, the "miracle synthetic" that Tam Lum points to in order to illustrate his origins to one of his many alter egos, Hong Kong Dream Girl (*Chickencoop* 8).

Despite the fluidity of Chinaman genealogy and identity, Chin nonetheless locates the majority of his fiction and his essays in California. However, Chin's decentering of geography and identity reinforces descriptions by Robert F. Gish and Gerald Haslam of California itself, not as a fixed geographic location, but rather as a continuing problem, an ontological question. The ongoing fluid construction of the state thus lays a shaky foundation for Chin that is irresolvably complex, yet historically, quite "western." As Chin writes in "This Is Not an Autobiography" (1985), the American west, both material and ideal, is as much a part of his history as it is of white Americans. Chin claims to have "mining, the Motherlode, the railroad, opera, outlaw and Kwan Kung in [his] blood and boyhood. [. . .] And the American west is mine. The US Interstate Freeway system. The railroad. THE LONE RANGER is a very Cantonese kind of hero" (109, 116). Chin makes such proprietary claims on the west not only in his criticism, but also in his earliest fiction; the Lone Ranger in fact makes an appearance in *The Chickencoop Chinaman* as the spokesman for white desire, accusing Chinese Americans of being "runaways from their place in the American dream [. . .] the West ain't big enough for the both of us" (38).

CHIN'S MAJOR WORKS

The Chickencoop Chinaman (1972) and The Year of The Dragon (1974)

Chin gained the acclaim of many critics and reviewers—and raised the hackles of at least as many—with his first two plays, which were produced at New York's American Place Theatre. *The Chickencoop Chinaman* and *The Year of The Dragon* set the stage for investigations of the complex terms of Asian American history, interethnic and intergenerational conflict, genealogy, and identity that would continue to dominate Chin's critical and fictional work. Most significantly, the two plays treat these various terms *as* questions, and suggest that it is his experiments with various notions of Asian American identity that largely established Chin as a contentious voice, the target of so much critical animosity in the decades to follow.

While shuttling between dream sequences and encounters between characters on a sparse set, *The Chickencoop Chinaman* traces Tam Lum's journey from Oakland, California, to Pittsburgh's black ghetto, Oakland, on a quest for a father figure to replace his own emasculated and absent father. Saturating the background of this short play are problematic claims about the hybridity of Asian American history and identity and the injunction of Tam's grandmother to listen for the trains, especially the mytho-historic Iron Moonhunter locomotive, that are his inheritance. Tam encounters a number of possible father figures, among them professional boxer Ovaltine Jack Dancer, Dancer's purported father Charley Popcorn, and the Lone Ranger, all of whom appear within the context of collapsing boundaries between the fictional and the actual, the mass mediated and the experiential. The problems raised by these father figures ultimately reinforce for Tam his need to negotiate for himself the tensions between various components of an identity that cannot ever be claimed as self-evident.

The play's first act centers on Tam's arrival in Pittsburgh to stay with his childhood friend, Blackjap Kenji, while he tracks down Charley Popcorn. The act opens with a fantasized encounter between Tam and "a dream monster from a popular American song of the twenties," the Hong Kong Dream Girl, who attempts to locate and concretize Tam's Chinese American identity. The conversation that follows is among Chin's most accomplished pieces of wordplay around identity, for Tam deflects Dream Girl's attempts to stabilize him as he continues to locate his identity, history, and genealogy in languages of synthesis and hybridity. Going through "voice and accent changes" all the while (6), Tam parries her questions about where and when he was born, to conclude:

> I am the natural born ragmouth speaking the motherless bloody tongue. No real language of my own to make sense with, so out comes everybody else's trash that don't conceive [. . .].
> Born? No! Crashed! Not born Stamped! Not born! Created! Not born. No more born than the heaven and earth. No more born than nylon or acrylic. For I am a Chinaman! A miracle synthetic! Drip dry and machine washable.
> I speak nothing but the mother tongues bein' born to none of my own, I talk the talk of orphans. (7-8; sic)

The rest of the act focuses on similar exchanges between characters as they attempt to read and interpret each other according to existing racial/ethnic paradigms. Tam's conception of his own identity is emphasized throughout as one formed primarily in language; and this is a conception that spills over and affects all the characters who will come into contact with him over the course of the play. The confrontational, and often invasive or offensive stance Tam immediately assumes when dealing with Kenji, Kenji's sometime partner Lee, and her son Robbie, is his vehicle of choice for continually testing multiple possible languages and identities against the foils of various characters and the ethnic, gender, and generational positions they represent for him. The second act opens like the first, with a dream sequence: here, Tam and Kenji encounter their childhood hero and father figure, the Lone Ranger, who enters the stage on a toy horse and appears as an aging, drug-addicted racist. The Lone Ranger reprimands the young men for seeking experiences outside their ethnic enclaves, for becoming "runaways from their place in the American dream [. . .] not thanking the masked man," the representative of white paternalism (38). Exiting, he curses Tam and Kenji with honorary whiteness, which Tam will later identify in Lee's estranged husband, Tom, as "anti-Chinaman vision" (60), the desire to reject the disruptive history of "Chinamans"; the curse, Tam concludes, "deafened my ear for trains all my boyhood long" (38). Later, Tam and Kenji find Popcorn, and in the course of asking him to participate in the documentary film about his son, Popcorn convinces Tam and Kenji that he is not Dancer's father at all, but had simply discovered an adolescent Dancer and trained him as a fighter. The search for genealogical legitimacy—whether by blood or proxy—thus turns out to be as much Dancer's fictional construct as it has been for Tam or Kenji. Recognizing the links between Dancer and himself, Tam's reflections on his one-time avatar comment reflexively on the broader concerns of the play itself. He considers reconfiguring the biography he set out to film and appears to shift focus subtly from Dancer to himself: "Make up some hokey connection between faking up a father, not knowing the past, and the killer instinct. But he's an old man now. Trusts me. I've failed all the old men that ever trusted me. Sold 'em out, watched 'em die, lost their names and been . . . been what? [. . .] What've I been for that?" (62).

However, the betrayal that Tam seems unable to resist or refuse does not stand as the play's last word. As the lights fade, Tam stands alone on stage acknowledging and, moreover, even celebrating the multiple inheritances that contributed to the moment in which he finds himself. Appropriating a longstanding Chinaman history that relies on theft and blood, Sierra railroad and Oakland Chinatown, myth and history, the play closes with an affirmation of the synthesis and hybridity that the Lone Ranger had cursed Tam to forget. The closing monologue is thus a reflection on the complexities of ethnic and linguistic origins with which the play had opened: "[I]n the beginning there was the Word! Then there was me! And the Word was CHINAMAN. And then there was me" (6).

The Year of the Dragon followed close on *Chickencoop* and serves in significant ways as its companion piece. Intensely domestic, the play shifts from a cramped San Francisco Chinatown apartment to brief glimpses of Fred Eng performing his Chinatown tour guide patter, a stereotypical pidgin English that is punctuated and undercut by the expletives Fred launches under his breath at his clients. The arrival of Fred's sister and her white husband, Ross, forces a collapse of the division between street and home on which Fred depends for stability. Significantly, Ross' first words of greeting are spoken in Chinese, to which Fred responds out of habit only to reconsider in midsentence: "'Goong hay fot . . .' Why am I saying this in my own house?" (73). As in *Chickencoop*, language quickly takes on an incendiary power: when Sis and Ross attempt to persuade Fred (a would-be novelist) to ghost write cookbooks and newspaper columns for their burgeoning—but nonetheless fake—"Mama Fu Fu" Chinese food and culture industry, Fred laments: "I'm going to write the great Chinese American Cookbook [. . .] MAMA FU FU'S RICE DEEM SUM right up their ass, cuz no one's going to read the great Chinese American novel" (83).

The invasion of Sis and Ross is the first indication that the apartment cannot remain Fred's point of safety and stability; instead it becomes the site for his utter destabilization as Pa's first wife, China Mama (who has been sitting quietly on stage to this point), begins to assert herself as Fred's mother. Fred is gradually trapped between the demands of the two immigrants, China Mama and Pa, that he acknowledge this originary relationship and "Be Chinese now," and of third-generation Ma, who reminds him that he is an "'American of Chinese Descent' like Jade Snow Wong, Hiram Fong, and Don Kingman" (92). Pa shortly announces to the gathered family that he has been made Mayor of Chinatown, and he dismisses out of hand former English major Fred for Ross, who suggests a Charlie Chan joke when asked to help with Pa's New Year parade speech. The tension between Ross and Fred is especially critical, as it illustrates Pa's almost automatic willingness to defer to Ross. Furthermore, the exchange and implied comparison between the two "sons" establishes the tonal counters that define Fred and his brother-in-law, the latter of whom sadly lives up to his character note: "Mattie's China-crazy white husband. Aesthetic, supercilious, Mr. Nice Guy" (69), and becomes a representative of "racist love," a quality long critiqued by Chin.

The remainder of the play focuses on Fred's efforts to take Ma and his younger brother, Johnny, out of Chinatown. Fred's demands that the family escape to the east coast are complicated by his own need to face his fears about leaving the life that is gradually consuming him, because it is the only life he knows intimately and from which he derives comfort in his daily experiences of humiliation, anger, and hatred. As much as he despises his life in Chinatown and the Charlie Chan tour guide act on which he depends for survival, the anxiety about being free to pursue his dream of writing is, itself, daunting. The Chinese New Year parade passes under the Eng family window as Fred encounters Pa, Ma, Johnny, Sis, Ross, and China Mama, and through them their numerous competing perceptions of life—and death—in Chinatown. In the midst of this competition, Pa dies before he has a chance to leave the apartment and give his speech, and the play closes with Fred and Johnny straining—literally over the dead body that is still in the room—against the rage they feel as they attempt once again to perform their Chinatown tour patter.

The Chinaman Pacific and Frisco R.R. Co. (1988)

This volume is a collection of Chin's shorter works of fiction that appeared between 1970 and 1988. Although they are too episodic to comprise a novel, the stories are nonetheless loosely connected by the experiences of Chinese American Dirigible from childhood through late middle age. "Railroad Standard Time" is Chin's opening gambit in which he returns to the railroad that played such a significant thematic role in *Chickencoop*. The story prefaces the themes of the entire collection, especially as it questions from the outset the ability of Chinese Americans to access a stable inheritance that could pass seamlessly from one generation to the next. The piece centers on Dirigible's inheritance of the "railroad standard all the way" watch of his grandfather, one of the first Chinese immigrants to work on the trains (1). Although Dirigible expects the watch to represent for him both generational and ethnic transmission of identity, the watch loses its power to keep inheritance's time despite its being Dirigible's mother claims, "the best" of the railroad watches her father had collected. A failure, as it is "[t]wo jewels short of new railroad standard and an outlaw watch" (2), the gift nonetheless successfully communicates a history that ties him to a communal experience: "I held it in one hand and then the other, hefted it, felt out the meaning of 'the best,' words that rang of meat and vegetables, oils, things we

13

touched, smelled, squeezed, washed, and ate, and I turned the big cased thing over several times" (2).

Dirigible takes the watch from his mother, claiming, whether despite or because of its failure to clearly demarcate time and identity: "This one was mine. No other" (2). Throughout the stories that follow, Dirigible is simultaneously motivated and thwarted by his desire for a clear sense of ethnic and national identity. The final piece in the collection, "The Sons of Chan," traces a middle-aged Dirigible's arrival in Las Vegas with a dual agenda: first, to assassinate the last white man to play Charlie Chan, and second, to track down Tempest Star, a stripper who stayed at a hotel where his mother had worked decades earlier. The story is presented as a report to an unspecified government for which Dirigible appropriates the narrative voice of effective and powerful Chinese American identity as he picks up the trail of Charlie Chan: "Suddenly the secret Chickencoop Chinaman was in town and on the case, when a moment before I was just Charlie Chan's son come to Las Vegas to hustle up a little nostalgia and a few extra bucks" (139). That clear sense of purpose and identity Dirigible expects the voice to provide him is ultimately exposed as a false front, however; Dirigible says to Chan in his Chickencoop Chinaman persona, "I was alert, Pop, a killer, and completely off-guard" (148). The identity of the cold-blooded killer that Dirigible would appropriate is itself exposed as part of a history of excess, a history of over-identification that draws him toward the various "war songs" that would center him and give him direction:

> I have no needs. No wants. I come from flaming names. From Chinamen who were too many for women. Too much get a move on for friendships. We each of us have our war songs to protect us. I sang mine often. Charlie Chan is my father. I am Charlie Chan's Number One Son. I am given to Charlie Chan's death. Then the Sons will be free. (150)

Dirigible finds himself caught between two stereotypes that Chin would later describe as the models of acceptable perversion and unacceptable perversion, each of which are simultaneously fascinating and repulsive both to Chin's characters and to American culture at large. Dirigible is unable to kill Chan, unable to succeed either in his mission of hero worship or of hero destruction, both of which amount to the same thing. Indeed, as he recalls the lyrics of "Hong Kong Dream Girl" at the moment of his failure, he concludes: "I'd never spoken anything but the sacred words of somebody's spiritual ritual to you, never gotten out of the motion of somebody's magic plot. [. . .] I don't not like the song enough to give it up" (161). His failure is only attenuated by his desire to reassert the Chickencoop Chinaman identity at the next opportunity: "I have nothing but failure to report from Las Vegas. Charlie Chan's Number One Son remembers a lot of failure. I am a legendary failure in America. I am a loved one, the chosen of the Charlie Chan chosen people. Pop, I will find you. I will be a hero of my people. Gee whiz, Pop, have I got a surprise for you" (165).

Chinaman Pacific thus comes full circle, ending with the same note of desire on which it began. In "Railroad Standard Time," Dirigible recognizes the fault lines between his desire for a stable inheritance and his realization of the flaws in a watch that is "two jewels short of railroad standard" (2). In "Sons of Chan," he experiences tension between his dream of assassinating Charlie Chan and his actual encounter with his target. These shifting signs of inheritance ultimately mark him as an outlaw. Provocatively, however, Dirigible takes possession of his failed inheritance; of the outlaw watch he claims, "I wouldn't give it back or trade it for another out of the collection. This one was mine. No other" (2). Dirigible fails doubly, through the watch and through his mission to assassinate Charlie Chan, to fix an identity; instead he finds himself located between "immigrant" and "native" cultures and cultural perceptions.

Throughout these stories Chin raises the stakes of the ongoing debates around ethnic American identity, asking through Dirigible's experiences whether the desire to retain the hold on a stable identity, however repulsive, is ultimately more attractive than the alternative of abandoning one's hold on those various anchors. Dirigible's lifelong encounter with loss—of the illocatability of his history—brings the reader herself full circle to the impossibility of tracing inheritance and identity as any sort of totality or plenitude. By recognizing the impossibility of abandoning the stereotype alongside the need to identify with it—a double recognition which is further supplemented with the unstable Chinaman identity—Chin strikes out toward a transformative, hybrid sense of Asian American identity. Thus, when Dirigible is left by his wife, he illustrates that hybridity by promising to be "more than quiet [. . .]. I won't be likable anymore" (3). Simultaneously acknowledging and resisting dominant stereotypes that limit his response to perversions of normative masculinity, Dirigible will no longer be contained on the dual personality grid, which allows only two possible alternatives for Asian American men: the perverse passivity of Charlie Chan, or the perverse vitality of Fu Manchu.

Donald Duk (1991)

The eponymous character from Chin's first published novel appears, in significant ways, as a younger and updated version of *Chickencoop*'s Tam Lum. As the novel opens shortly before Chinese New Year celebrations begin in San Francisco, eleven-year-old Donald is plagued by his perception of an absence of legitimate or adequate models on which he might form his own cultural and linguistic identity. In order to escape from the quotidian reality of Chinatown life, Donald spends much of his time at a dance studio owned by the "Chinese Fred Astaire" and watching old movies on TV, hoping for a time when he can "live the late night life in old black-and-white movies and talk with his feet like Fred Astaire, and smile Fred Astaire's sweet lemonade smile" (1). As Shawn Wong describes the novel's opening: "All [Donald] knows growing up in [. . .] Chinatown is that it hardly resembles 'America' at all" (15). However, the failure of Chinatown to meet Donald's standards is founded not on any failure attributable to Chinatown itself, but rather on Donald's acceptance of dominant perceptions of, and limitations on, the possibilities for Chinese American identity. Like other Chin characters, he is caught in the demand that he accept either a positively construed assimilatory identity or a negatively construed separatist one.

When Donald's namesake, the Cantonese opera star Uncle Donald, visits the Duk family to celebrate Donald's twelfth birthday, he is able to recognize "how that snooty private school you go to has pulled the guts out of you and turned you into some kind of engineer of hate for everything Chinese [. . .]. You blame every Chinese who ever lived, everything Chinese you ever heard of for the way white kids act like fools when they hear your name" (23). While Uncle Donald identifies this hatred in Donald's theft of a model airplane from a collection that represents the 108 heroes of Shi Nai'An's fourteenth-century chronicle, *Water Margin* (*Outlaws of the Marsh*), on the night of his theft Donald himself comes into contact with the first in a procession of other possible modes of Chinese American identity, when he encounters a traumatized Vietnam veteran, the "American Cong" Victor Lee, on the roof of his apartment.

Although American Cong is not caught up in the desire for visibility—specifically for whiteness—in which Donald finds himself, he nonetheless appears as a foreshadowing of the trauma inherent in the desire for identification. As he speaks with Donald he recalls first his time being lost among the Montagnards in Vietnam, where the distinctions between time and space, the familiar and the foreign, collapse: "They grow corn! Just like in Iowa. Corn! Here I am, no dog tags, no jewelry. No wallets. No labels. No patches. No insignia. Climb and hide for days to get to the Montagnards. And I crawl into a cornfield on the side of a motherin' mountain! [. . .] I'm home again!" (19). However, the survival strategy of anonymity or of disidentification Cong is able to practice in Vietnam fails to translate when he returns to the United States, his ostensible home. Among other returned veterans he becomes too visible; he looks "too much like Charlie to them. Too many come back crazy to dink a dink when they come back [. . .]. Crazies who are still fighting the war they lost, man. [. . .] So I'm here [in Chinatown] getting lost where everybody looks like Charlie and nobody expects to find Americans" (19).

As his birthday nears, Donald dreams nightly about the history of his Chinese immigrant forebears working on the railroad in the Sierras, then spends his days at the library researching the events that led to the completion of the first transcontinental railroad. He begins to engage with the tension between the lived history of the Chinese in America, which is only accessible in his dreams, and the dominant portrayal of that history by his teacher, Mr. Meanwright, who depends on the devaluation and excision of Chinaman contributions to give America its seamless, whitewashed appearance. Donald must eventually go public with his experiences, first by sharing his dreams in order to salvage his relationships with his family and his best friend, and later by admitting to his theft of the airplane to save Victor Lee from being framed for a Chinatown murder. Both events depend on a blend of histories: not only does Donald discover and divulge the facts of contemporary and historical Chinese American experiences, he also encounters the history of myths and legends that inform and sometimes mirror the events of his dreaming and waking lives, which, themselves, begin to lose their distinction.

What Donald ultimately realizes as he explores the history of Chinese people in America and begins to experience Chinese American culture as a participant rather than as a disdainful observer, is his ability to engage in the continual development of his multiple, and not always compatible, cultural inheritances; and, moreover, he begins to recognize the fluidity of his local culture as a specifically American trait. The hypermasculine persona that *Chinaman*'s Dirigible had earlier appropriated and believed in as a model for seamless identification is reassessed in *Donald Duk*, acknowledged as a strategic front that comes, King Duk suggests, not from any uniform or identifiable inheritance, but from an ability to accept the hybridity and transience of identity and to find strength in that knowledge. Countering Donald's desire for whiteness—or for an impossible deracination—King Duk claims:

> I think Donald Duk may be the very last American-born Chinese-American boy to believe you have to give up being Chinese to be an American [. . .]. The new Chinese immigrants prove that. [. . .] Instead of giving anything up, they add on. They're including American in everything else they know. And that makes them stronger than any of the American-born, like me, who had folks who worked hard to know absolutely nothing about China, who believed that if all they knew was 100 percent American-made in the USA Yankee know howdy doodle dandy, people would not mistake them for Chinese. (42)

It is significant that this analysis comes from Donald's father, who was not an immigrant himself, but rather the grandson of immigrants; King's parents, however, were among those who believed the most desirable Chinese American subject position was achieved through precisely the disidentification with ethnicity that their grandson would ultimately desire. Although it is only alluded to briefly, King Duk was driven to radically revisit—and to radically reinvent—his ethnic history by running away from San Francisco's Chinatown to Hong Kong to join a Cantonese opera troupe. He returns to Chinatown by choice, not through the necessity of having never experienced anything outside the ethnic preserve it demarcates. While Chin's themes and concerns remain relatively constant, his first novel is, nonetheless, a significant departure from his other literary and critical work, since its protagonist is not on the irreparably mournful, doomed search for genealogical or ethnic legitimacy found in his early plays and short stories, nor is the novel another illustration of the savvy, street smart Chinatown Cowboy image Chin has developed as his essayist's persona. The rage that saturates his earlier work remains in Donald, and in other members of the Duk family; but it seems that the adolescent protagonist offers more promise than the young—but far from youthful—characters that populate his other literary and critical work. Chin does not locate Donald's potential for transformation in a successful performance of earlier protagonists' efforts to clearly identify themselves historically, ethnically, or otherwise. Rather, Donald's ability to tentatively place himself in the matrix of subject positions that Chinatown both offers and requires becomes a point of departure, not a point of stability. Indeed, as Donald's father cautions the gathering of Duk and Azalea families on the eve of the last day of Chinese New Year celebrations, "Life is war [. . .]. You want to keep your know-how and build more know-how with it, not get hung up admiring what you made and get all sentimental about it" (157).

Gunga Din Highway (1994)

Chin's longest and most complex work of fiction to date is *Gunga Din Highway*, an encyclopedic assessment and critique of late modern and contemporary Asian American experience. The novel is narrated by four Chinese American men as they move from postwar youth through late middle age, and each of these men represents a particular position on or experience of Asian American identity. The ostensible son of Chinese immigrant Longman Kwan and his fourth-generation Chinese American wife Hyacinth, Ulysses Kwan is the novel's primary narrator, whose experiences with and reflections on history, literature, and politics closely mirror Chin's own. Furthermore, the quest for legitimacy and identity through genealogy that is pursued by many of Chin's fictional characters is replayed through the tense relationship between Ulysses and his estranged father. As in other Chin narratives, as well, genealogy is presented here through complicated relations of blood and fantasy, desires for legitimacy and history that often stand at cross purposes to each other.

Indeed, much of the strain in Ulysses' and Longman's relationship—between the son's self-invented identity and the father's goal of assimilation—arises from Longman's desire to attain in reality the part he plays in the movies as Charlie Chan's Number Four Son, the Chinaman Who Dies. Although Longman is Chinese born, he claims a unique status as the most "Americanized" of all the Sons of Chan, and thus as Chan's most legitimate son. He promises his wife that for the sake of his sons he will become the "first Chinese to play Charlie Chan in the movies" (13). When Hyacinth balks at setting such an example for the next generation, Longman counters:

> As Charlie Chan I shall lead you to your great salvation. For, it is written: As God the Father gave up a son in the image of the perfect white man, to lead whites to walk the path of righteousness toward salvation, and praise God, so the White Man gave up a son in the image of the perfect Chinese American to lead the yellows to build the road to

acceptance toward assimilation. Ah, sweet assimilation. Charlie Chan was his name. (13)

Ulysses is, himself, as much the product of Asian American fantasy as of Chinese and Chinese American blood, and he inherits through this complex genealogy, if not the desire, then the demand from those around him to live as the Grandson of Charlie Chan. Ulysses spends much of his life resisting the road toward assimilation on which his father has set him; he chooses, instead, to reach back into Chinaman history first by identifying with Chinese history and mythology as a child, and later by becoming a brakeman on the Southern Pacific and Western Pacific railroads. Through these various identifications, Ulysses is able to live the hybrid experience his immigrant friend, Ben Han, would later identify as the greatest lesson they learned from their Chinese school teacher: "Unlike anyone else in the world, we were neither Chinese nor American. All things were possible. No guilt. We were pure self-invention" (93).

Despite the lesson about self-invention from the Horse, the dominant narrative about the role Chinese Americans are to play is clear to everyone around Ulysses, white or Asian. A brief episode from Ulysses' childhood illustrates the narrative's pervasiveness: when Ulysses explains to the old men in the park that he is leaving the confines of Oakland's Chinatown to see *East of Eden*, "a Movie About Me," the men counter, "Movie about you? Any movie about you, you die!" (105). Thus faced with a narrative that is so dominant it has taken on the contours of reality, as Ulysses grows older, he begins to disrupt the narrative not through opposition, but by making it short circuit its own prejudices and preconceptions about race and ethnicity. Ulysses spends his late twenties shuttling between ethnic fantasies, between appearing on Bay Area TV as the "Power-to-the-People Minister of Education of the Chinatown Vanguard of the Third World Revolution—the

Chinatown Black Tigers" (218), and ghostwriting a play, *Fu Manchu Plays Flamenco*, for his childhood friend, Ben Mo. Simultaneously tracing and parodying Chin's own experiences of the 1970s, Ulysses becomes "a conscious and knowing clown" (218), as *Fu Manchu Plays Flamenco* plays in New York at "The American Face Theatre." The event reunites Ulysses' childhood friends and makes them in the public eye, as Diego Chang recalls, "the ornamental Orientals of the minute. I know it. Ulysses knows it. Ben knows it. No problem" (254). Thematically and historically the play reflects Chin's early work, and it too provokes hostile reactions from both assimilationist and separatist cadres of Asian Americans. When a Chinese American gang leader attempts to shut the play down for performing stereotypes of Asian Americans, Diego narrates as Ulysses explains the potential for disruption that is effected in a critically motivated repetition of the stereotypes:

> "Have you ever heard of satire?" Ulysses asks Tom Tom Tom and the Dragon Kings. Ulysses is crazy. What is he doing, dressed up as Fu Manchu, standing up to a Chinatown gang for his right to sing "Ching Chong Chinaman sitting on a rail/Along come a choo-choo train and cut off his tail" . . . ? So what is he doing?
>
> "Satire is when you make fun of how *they* think and what *they* say in order to make *them* look *stupid*," Ulysses said, not too slow, not too fast. I don't know if he makes them understand, but he keeps them listening until the fight fizzles out. (257)

However, as was the case for *Chickencoop* and *Year*, even the favorable responses appear, to Ulysses, to miss the point. In fact, when Ben becomes involved with a rising Chinese American author, Pandora Toy, and attempts to argue that her autobiographical novel, *Neurotic Exotic Erotic Orientoxic*, is doing the same thing as the play, Ulysses explodes. Ben claims that the play and the novel both describe Chinese American cultures that are accessible and acceptable to whites; of the play, he states: "We are revealing the truth of the Chinese culture we reject and creating a Chinese-American culture that is more humane, more considerate of women" (261). Ulysses, however, distinguishes between the real and the fake—the distinction between conceding to and disrupting white stereotypes that has been central to Chin's work; he claims, contrary to Ben, that "*Fu Manchu Plays Flamenco* is creating a Chinese American culture that kicks white racism in the balls with a shit-eating grin" (261).

As the events of the novel slip into the early 1990s, Ulysses continues to appreciate such short-circuiting moves. Capitalizing on the inability of white people to take Asian Americans seriously, he has become a writer of Zombie movies for the Four Horsemen of Hollywood, something that none of the black leaders of the 1960s could have done. "I mean," Ulysses explains, "no one in Hollywood is about to give Eldridge, Huey, or Stokely a job writing zombie movies. [. . .] They are trapped in the little moment of history they made because people take them seriously" (345). Nonetheless, at the request of the studio, Ulysses transforms his personal political experiences into *Night of the Living Third World Dead*, a film in which Orpheus raises the dead from Arlington National Cemetery:

> Malcolm X, Martin Luther King, freedom riders long forgotten in unmarked graves, the consciences, the folksingers, and memories of the '60s, and all my brothers and sisters of the Third World Revolution Power to the People politics from the barrel-of-a-gun days have been secretly buried in Arlington by the FBI for the usual FBI reasons of patriotism and paranoid schizo banzai gung ho arrogance and loyalty to the

Bureau. Now they all rise from the dead. Even if they're not dead yet, they all rise from the dead. (346)

Despite the admitted stupidity of the film, when the novel version of one of his screenplays appears, Ulysses tells his family at the wake for his father, "Everyone's reviewing *Third World Dead* as not just a serious Chinese American novel, but Ah-Sin, as the Chinaman man's answer to Pandora Toy" (363). The first meeting of Ulysses' entire family in years, the wake provides the scene for the exposure of various intimate, longstanding grievances and secrets. Most importantly, Ulysses is told the secret of the complicated transPacific, incestuous genealogy that has set the equally complicated plot of his life in motion.

Longman Kwan's death becomes a point at which many of the themes and events of the novel come together, however problematically. As he nears death, Longman imagines a restaging of a never-released film about a Chinese American bomber squad in World War Two, *Anna May Wong*, in which he had acted. The film's cast, however, appears to Longman as a collage of the Asian American actors with whom he had worked in the 1940s and 50s, along with classical Cantonese Opera characters, and all are dressed in their opera costumes as they take off on their mission to bomb a Russian oil field. Longman muses, "Cantonese opera has never seen anything like this" (381). To further complicate this collapse of multiple historical periods, the mythologies of Cantonese Opera and Hollywood film, Ulysses claims actually to see the plane roughly at the time of Longman's death: "It flies over me. I turn and watch it fly away toward LA. It must be the last B-24 in the world that still flies" (381). Through a procession of characters out of Ulysses' past, the funeral, too, replays the unstable blend of genealogies and experiences he has faced throughout his life. Most significantly, Longman's first son, Ulysses' China Brother Joe Joe, appears, followed by Anlauf Loraine, "the man who will continue to play Charlie Chan to Pa's Number Four Son on late-night cable TV movies forever," who is accompanied by Longman's fourth and fifth known sons (388). All are "dressed in white suits, white, the Chinese color of death, white, the white of Charlie Chan's white duck. The Charlie Chans wear Charlie Chan Panama straw hats" (388). As television news cameras roll, the old tongmen, "the ones who come out only for funerals of their own kind" (391), arrive and create a veritable standoff over the final representation of the man who, to the various gathered factions, represented both assimilation and separation. Like a reflection on Fred Eng's position at the conclusion of *Year of the Dragon*, this conflict over Longman's body also illustrates the tension of Ulysses' own contested position and inheritance.

Finally, the railroad emerges again as a critical force in the arsenal of metaphors Chin employs to recall, yet simultaneously disrupt, the inheritance of historical and ethnic experience. The novel's final chapter, "Home Terminal," raises and complicates the symbolic value of the railroad as it evokes the titular image of arrival and linearity, yet also traces the failure of these images to cohere into definitive meaning. Despite the evocation throughout the novel of quests and *Bildungsromane*—both Asian (-American) and European—the conclusion resists resolution as time and space are thrown out of joint when Diego Chang's housekeeper gives birth to a new generation of Chinamans. As Ulysses speeds across San Francisco toward the Chinatown hospital he finds himself returning to his days on the Southern Pacific railroad; he finds himself, in fact, dispersed through multiple times and spaces that contribute to the formation of Chinaman history. Recalling some three decades of Chin's points of reference, the mytho-historic Iron Moonhunter at last descends from the Sierras with Ulysses in the cab, feeling "the hundreds, the thousands of percussing children tumbling folk songs in the hollows of my bones [. . .] singing round the long curve past Port Costa" (402). Meanwhile, Ulysses' car travels through San Francisco, "along the streets where the trains used to run" (403).

The outcome of such a destabilized and detemporalized journey is not a return to coherence, a point of convergence of these lines of flight; it opens, rather, the possibility of rupturing the silence to which Asian Americans have been consigned. Ulysses claims of his journey: "The power brings me out of a bang, and I savor the shudder and growl scattering me across the country, and I fill more and more silence, and grow loud, and grow dense' (403). Such a movement is not positioned as the originary moment of a complete Asian American subjectivity. As he drives downtown, Ulysses ushers in a new generation of ruptured subjects, homeless in an atomized—scattered—ethnic American identity and history.

CRITICAL RECEPTION AND LITERARY/CULTURAL CRITICISM

From the outset, critical reception of Chin's work has been mixed; moreover, various and contradictory assessments have often been based on identical evidence: the sometimes unaccountable or unidentifiable sense of rage of Chin and his literary protagonists, the "black" street language, the unapologetic identification of popular culture racism, the critique of "Chinese American" culture and identity. Early critical difficulties in clearly establishing the impact or import of *The Chickencoop Chinaman* would be reflected in the similar challenges that faced responses to Chin as a creative writer, a cultural critic, and a public intellectual. Those difficulties, however, have kept Chin central to the field of Asian American literature because of the challenges he continues to pose therein; indeed, since the 1970s, many critics have used Chin as a surrogate for the entirety of postwar writing by Asian American men. Much of Chin's continued significance in the pantheon of

Asian American writers is due to the negative function he has come to serve in the academic field, as responses to his work often emphasize the real or perceived need to assign a moral value to their objects of study. Responding to broad critical strokes, which became increasingly consistent in their dismissiveness, Chin has produced a significant body of cultural and literary criticism that can help readers understand the ways in which he assesses his own work, as well as his position relative to past and present Asian American literature.

For many critics, in fact, Chin's work would serve as the line of demarcation between legitimate and illegitimate expressions of ethnicity, a line identified by, among others, Myron Simon in his *MELUS* essay, "Two Angry Ethnic Writers" (1976). In his response to presentations delivered by Chin and Ishmael Reed at a session of the Modern Language Association (MLA) convention, which were later published in the same issue of *MELUS*, Simon derided the authors' anger at the lack of critical attention afforded their work. Outlining the contours of his position in this still-unresolved debate, Chin argues in his response, "Afterward" (1976), that, however personal, anger is a force that can disrupt dominant demands for ethnic voices celebrating only tolerance, isomorphic intercultural translation, and assimilation to white notions of universality—celebrations that often proceed at the expense of confrontation and critique. Continuing, Chin claimed that the roots of his anger were more diffuse than those of Reed or other copanelists Thomas Sanchez and Karl Shapiro, because Asian American culture was misrepresented through the small body of literature that had been even marginally received in America. For the most part, Chin argued, he was "mad at the world that drove me away believing we'd never written anything at all, much less anything about yellows that would speak to me and bring my notions of great literature home" (16). As he recalls belatedly discovering a generation of

postwar Asian American writing in John Okada and Louis Chu, Chin explains his rage at thinking himself the "first," the solitary Asian American writer who would have to invent a literary language out of an absolute absence of predecessors' forms or models.
Shortly after the MLA conference that sparked the *MELUS* exchange, Chin became infamous for his outspoken analysis of Maxine Hong Kingston's novel/memoir, *The Woman Warrior* (1976), which he considered to be a vehicle for stereotypical portraits of Asians and Asian Americans. As he would later write in "Come All Ye Asian American Writers of the Real and the Fake" (1991), the novel reproduced and ultimately legitimated a longstanding injunction from white American culture for Asian Americans—and especially Asian American women—to "dump the Chinese race and make for white universality" (27). One of Chin's early essays, "Confessions of a Chinatown Cowboy" (1972), reprinted in *Bulletproof Buddhists*, investigated the history and effects of this injunction, and he began to develop there the hypermasculine public persona that became the base of so many of the dismissals of his work that followed, because that persona would be uncritically positioned as the stable foil to Kingston's equally stable "feminist" voice. Yet, in his own work, while researching characters for a television documentary, Chin recalls seeing himself as a self-consciously cheap imitation of activist Ben Fee, a "word of mouth legend, a bare-knuckled unmasked man, a Chinaman loner out of the old West, a character out of Chinese swordslingers, a fighter. The kind of Chinaman we've been taught to forget if we don't want America to drive Chinatown out of town" (*Bulletproof* 65-66). And, although Chin compares himself to Fee as "solid affectation" to the original model (67), he nonetheless proceeds to find enough commonality to speak with Fee: not from the stable ground of shared identity, but rather through the mutual recognition of the emptiness of stable and exclusionary conceptions

of identity. Chin writes, "We'd show in the talk whether we had anything to say to each other, other than 'whiter than thou,' 'more Chinese than thou,' 'more assimilated than thou'" (70). Indeed, Chin's meeting with Fee, and his assessment of this intergenerational standoff, sets the scene for his ongoing, broader assessments of the historic role of Asian America through the decades to follow. By the mid-1980s Chin appeared to have outstayed his welcome in the arenas of both Asian American literature specifically and contemporary American literature generally. Elaine Kim's response to "The Sons of Chan" (*Chinaman Pacific*), especially, marked the turning point on which the negative perception and dismissal of Chin and his work would achieve the status of an institutional commonplace for many critics to come. In Kim's essay, "'Such Opposite Creatures': Men and Women in Asian American Literature" (1990), Chin practically became a stand-in for the entirety of modern and postwar Asian American male writers, from Filipino American Carlos Bulosan (*America Is in the Heart* [1943]), to Japanese American John Okada (*No-No Boy* [1957]), to Chinese Americans Louis Chu (*Eat a Bowl of Tea* [1961]) and Jeffery Paul Chan ("Auntie Tsia Lays Dying" [1974]). In Kim's analysis, Chin represented the hyper-masculine Asian American writer who does not "[question] the legitimacy of patriarchy's closed universe [and seeks] the white male center for himself at the expense of women" (78). In "Confessions of a Chinatown Cowboy," however, one finds that Chin's notion of Asian American masculinity is asserted everywhere, yet clearly demarcated nowhere; if he does demand an assertive, masculine Chinaman persona, he also presents significant justification for that need through both historical and contemporary evidence that the popular conception of Asian American men has long been an emasculated one. Once Chin meets Fee, the essay becomes, in fact, a meditation on a national cultural effort to obliterate Chinese America through the extinction of its men: "The stereotype of us being a race without manhood has been so thoroughly and subtly suffused throughout American culture for so long that it's become a comfortable part of the American subconscious" (99). Because Chin's characters—as well as Chin himself—live in a world devoid of laudable Asian American male icons (besides Charlie Chan and Fu Manchu, who represent for Chin the acceptably perverse and unacceptably perverse subject positions that America is capable of seeing), they are faced with the burden of creating their own sense of masculinity.

It remains important to point out that Chin is neither an innocent victim of nor a passive target for the critics who dismiss his work; indeed, evidence for their criticism is there in abundance. Nonetheless, as we examine in depth the literary and cultural critical work Chin has produced since the 1970s, we find that the many dismissive voices overlook significant components of his thought and the aesthetic practices that accompany his thought. The greatest problem here is that later respondents eventually stopped reading Chin's work and instead accepted the excerpts employed by earlier critics as the totality of his work. Moreover, they have also written as though Chin's critical work responded to a larger body of literary and cultural production that lay outside the scope of its initial critique; for instance, when Patricia Chu extends the terms of Chin's response to *The Woman Warrior* as though it responded as well to Kingston's second novel, *Tripmaster Monkey* (1990), she imagines a stable and clear-cut field on which Chin and Kingston battle for domination over Asian American literature. Generally, too, readers have arrived in a peculiar position, especially since the early 1990s: while criticizing and dismissing Chin, they have expected to be excused from the responsibility of reading not only his critical work, but his fiction as well.

Two essays, "This Is Not an Autobiography" (1985) and "Come All Ye Asian American Writers of the Real and the Fake," became the touchstones to which critics would turn for years to illustrate their claims about Chin's masculinism, his historical chauvinism, and his anti-immigrant nativism. As Chin argues, throughout the history of European and American encounters with Asia and Asians, there have been significant efforts to replace various indigenous and immigrant histories and cultures of Asians with white fantasies about the "Orient" and "Orientals." Critics have often mistaken Chin's efforts at recovering the actually existing literary history of Asia and Asian America as a rejection of the artistic license to invent and imagine other possible experiences, identities, and the like. For Chin, however, neither register cancels out the other; rather, artistic invention and historical consciousness both retain critical importance and, at best, inform each other in Asian American literature. As he argues in "This Is Not an Autobiography," there is a significant relationship between his diffuse artistic articulations of identity and his accompanying demand to examine the historical tensions surrounding dominant calls for Chinese and Chinese American cultures to be either delegitimated or clearly contained and demarcated; moreover, Chin describes that relationship only provisionally: "Before I can make art of my yellow self, and play with my knowledge of Asian America, we have to come to some agreement about the facts of yellow history" ("This" 109). Thus, Chin conceives of and portrays history and historical reclamation in his essays not as the endpoint of Asian American experience, but as the foundation for the play and provocation that take center stage in his fiction.

Part of the contention around Chin's essays certainly arises from the polemic tone he takes to critique modern stereotypes and to demand a revisiting of Asian American history. His willingness to name names when forming his criticism is unnerving, and the specificity of his critique may account for the very personal and visceral response he elicits from his respondents. Although she is certainly the best known among literary circles, Kingston is, in fact, only one of many Asian American public figures who have come under fire from Chin. For example, as he writes of television shows and series in the 1970s and 1980s that continued to perpetuate historically false notions of treatment of, especially, Chinese women in America, Chin not only takes on the networks that aired the shows, but also the Asian Americans who acted in them and who actively defended the stereotypes. Turning to actor Robert Ito, who defended the depiction of Chinese America in the 1979 "China Doll" episodes of *How the West Was Won*, Chin claims:

> [H]e invented a new stereotype; he defended the departure from fact as being necessary to depict the "fact" that "there were abuses of women." He unabashedly referred to a racial stereotype to defend racial stereotyping, and nobody in the audience of Asian Americans flinched. Portraying Chinese culture as despicable, bashing the men, pitying and freeing the women, have become ends in themselves. ("Come" 28)

Nor, Chin continues, are Ito's comments defensible simply because the events were so far in the past that either the history is blurred beyond recognition or the contemporary liberatory message outweighs the significance of the actual past. The nineteenth- and early twentieth-century Chinese American history Chin presents to counter its reductive popular depiction is later supplemented by his extensive analysis of Japanese American internment during World War Two, in which he locates significant echoes of previous Chinese American experiences.

Foremost in his analysis, Chin traces the ways in which homogenizing formal and ideological moves in Chinese American literature served a broad cultural function, mapping out the territories of legitimate and illegitimate expressions of Asian American life. He documents the resurgence of these literary stereotype machines immediately prior to Japanese internment and their dominance long after the war's end, to the extent that the first autobiography to come out of the camps is "not very subtle proof that the American concentration camps were behavior modification programs that worked" (51). Chin claims that the Japanese American Citizens League (JACL) not only supported the idea of the camps, but also actually assisted in their planning with the War Relocation Authority, in order to achieve their long term assimilationist goals. A new literary movement, informed by longstanding stereotypes of Japan and Japanese culture, was the vehicle of choice through which the JACL would encourage all Japanese Americans to abandon their cultural inheritance for assimilation. Erasing already-existing literary traditions and movements, many writers "'abandoned' Japanese American history, turned rabidly against the Issei and Japanese culture, and fantasized about joyous acculturation, righteous white acceptance" (52). The fact that Japanese American protest literature only appeared in brief flashes during and after World War Two, and never received significant attention, reinforced the notion that there was no Japanese American (literary) history worth preserving. As Chin writes, Japanese American opposition to the JACL's support of assimilationist programs—James Omura's Heart Mountain Fair Play Committee, for instance—was consigned to oral history because the JACL and their agenda controlled, at least ideologically, "the writing of Japanese American news, Japanese American history, Japanese American fiction, and Japanese American poetry" (54). As he continues, the "resistance faded into the oral tradition of those Nisei and Issei the JACL-dominated Japanese Americans called 'vengeful and vindictive.' What was 'nothing they dared tell' became nothing at all" (54).

Chin's lengthy introduction to *The Big Aiiieeeee!* (1991) thus links two disparate levels, the historical and the literary, on which

Chinese American and Japanese American histories are told, and through those two levels, he continues to mark out the territories of the "real" and the "fake" which have been the source of so much critical backlash against his work. In fact, he traces the contentious history of history-making for Asians in America as a battle between dominant forces that would continue to invest in a static, stereotype-driven history of Asian Americans and the minor, creative forces that continue to be informed by, yet simultaneously transform, Asian and American history and experience as living forces. Chin's twin roles as an artist and as a literary-historical critic make contact through his analyses precisely because the history he covers is, predominantly, a monolithic literary history that has become institutionalized and taken the place of other possible histories of Asian America.

Chin balances his criticism of individual public figures in Asian America with illustrations of early Asian American experiences that give lie to still-powerful stereotypes. Among his most provocative examples, Chin points to the development of family associations, "tongs," in the United States to dissect three commonly held stereotypes about Chinese America Citing the 1876 bylaws of the Lung Kong Tin Yee Association, Chin demonstrates that Chinese immigrants were not simply "sojourners" who never desired residency and citizenship in America; rather, they proceeded through the legal processes that would establish their permanent presence. The bylaws work against the perception that "we came to rob America of its wealth and go back to China, another life" ("Afterward" 17). Secondly, the Association printed a pamphlet "making its pitch to new members by using what is unforgettable to anyone who was a Chinese child, the stuff of pop cults, comic books, and personal honor," primarily, *The Romance of the Three Kingdoms* (32). This appeal demonstrates that Chinese immigrants brought their culture and their literary traditions with them; and, rather than forgetting their historical and mythological traditions, they created in the tongs, according to Chin, "new art born of new experiences and informed by the ethics of the heroic tradition in Asian childhood literature and myth" (30). Finally, and most importantly, the new art Chin describes in the encounters and conflicts between Chinese and American people and cultures resulted in the transformation of the forms, beliefs, and values that were held by both. A hybrid, impermanent culture arose from such encounters, as it does from ongoing immigrations, and thus America continues to develop not as a monolithic totality, but rather as a "depot, a marketplace." As Chin would claim in a later essay, "Rashomon Road" (1997), "What we called American culture, like the language, was a pidgin, marketplace culture" (295).

Moreover, the historical and present experiences of (Asian-) American hybridity belie the most pernicious myth of the "dual personality identity crisis," in which Asian Americans must choose between opposing and mutually exclusive "Asian" and "American" cultural and linguistic identities. Chin exposes the belief that one simply chooses between separatism and assimilation, between yellow and white, as illusory and self-destructive, because such a choice has never been possible. Nonetheless, as Chin continues, it has been posed as the choice that Asian Americans must make: "The conflict between the heathen and Christian, the Chinaman and the honorary white, the despicable pariah and the acceptable pariah, the either/or dual personality and identity crisis feeds and flashes on the self-hatred of the mutually repugnant halves of the self in a kind of perpetual motion" (25). Chin points out that such stereotypes, both of the Chinaman who refuses the open arms of America and of the assimilated Chinese American who rejects the potential richness of hybridity for the monoculture, have been the two historically preferred visions of Asian America; and the reason he singles Kingston out of contemporary Asian American writers is because her immense popularity—a popularity calculatedly generated by the generic moniker of "autobiography/memoir" that accompanied *The Woman Warrior*—allowed a rich and diverse Chinese American cultural history to be replaced by Kingston's narrator's fantasies about both China and America. While Kingston and her narrator may express the problems of intercultural transmission quite provocatively, the larger problem raised by the autobiography/memoir tag is that her story comes to stand in for history (see, for instance, Li, *Imagining* 51-52). Some fifteen years later, Chin writes: "Fake work breeds fake work. David Henry Hwang repeats Kingston's revision of Fa Mulan and Yue Fei, and goes on to impoverish and slaughter Fa Mulan's family to further dramatize the cruelty of the Chinese. [. . .] This version of history is their contribution to the stereotype" (3).

Although Chin is, himself, no stranger to postmodernist or other avant-garde formal and narrative approaches in his fiction, he does not present the arguments of his fiction as accurate representations of his—or any—Chinese American history, nor has anyone taken them as such. However, when Kingston's or Hwang's works come to take the place of Chinese American history, particular key scenes became perpetuated as the actual history of both China and Chinese America. With no little prescience then, Chin's aspiring writer Fred Eng suggests that literary forms—the cookbook, the travelogue, and especially the autobiography—may be, of themselves, restrictive, and those forms are often a vehicle for the perpetuation of destructive stereotypes, and are, only rarely, the grounds on which disruptive strategies are performed. The question for Chin becomes, then, how the marginal writer might engage with dominant images, metaphors, or forms of writing in a way that would resist recuperation into normative notions of ethnic identity; thus, Chin is able to argue that his own autobiographical references in *Gunga Din Highway* function as "lures," and not in an isomorphic relationship between literary and historical discourses. On the other hand, the perpetuation of black hat/white hat polar opposition on which Kingston places China and America in *The Woman Warrior* may set the scene for moments of subversion, yet that fundamentally static relationship is easily recuperated into what Sau-Ling Cynthia Wong would later call the "sugar sisterhood" of white feminist readers who prefer a steady diet of ethnic mother-daughter stories and their attendant "quasi-ethnographic Orientalist discourse" (181). If we return to Chin's earlier essays we see, in fact, a similar critique that predates Kingston's first novel; for instance, in "Racist Love" (1972), Chin and Jeffery Paul Chan write: "The ideal racial stereotype is a low maintenance engine of white supremacy whose efficiency increases with age, as it becomes 'authenticated' and 'historically verified'" (66).

It is particularly in the face of present dismissal that David Leiwei Li illustrates an "institutional ignorance" of Chin's work in general, and claims that "an evaluation of his role as a historic agent becomes indispensable," because Chin's relegation to a position outside of legitimate Asian American writing indicates a broader disciplinary process of "effacing the oppositional" ("Formation" 211). As Li argues, Chin's historical significance as part of the early-contemporary avant-garde of ethnic American writing is important in its own right; moreover, as Chin continues to write both fiction and criticism, his presence as a contentious figure in Asian American literature and literary studies also demands ongoing attention. His latest collection of essays, *Bulletproof Buddhists* (1998), illustrates the ways in which he has continued to develop and work over the concerns—material and ideal, fictional and historical—at the heart of Asian American experience. Because Chin thus remains a vital, living producer of and respondent to contemporary Asian American literature and culture, it should not be surprising that Li, in his book *Imagining the Nation* (1998), uses Chin as a sounding board for his analysis of the corpus of post-1970 Asian American literary production.

The American cultural landscape to which Chin constantly refers remains, like his favored metaphors of the highway, the railroad, and the marketplace, transient and impermanent, and such impermanence obtains despite the historical artifacts to which he polemically turns as the foundations of an authentic Asian American voice. Thus, a movement and a tension between claims of authenticity and their constant disruption saturate Chin's work and develop multiple subject positions—past, present, future—of ethnic Asians in the United States. What Chin would discover in a meeting with Ben Fee, the prototype for Chin's own Chinatown Cowboy persona, is an opportunity to form a different, hybrid language, one that resists being appropriated and repackaged as the sole, transcendent form or voice of authenticity. Concluding his first interview with Fee, Chin states: 'Thanks Ben. Ride with this Chinatown cowboy a bit while I run off to rustle strange words and maverick up a language to write this mess in" (*Bulletproof* 71).

Primarily, Chin has since the early 1970s analyzed the language games that have themselves grounded much of the critical dismissal with which he has been faced, and he emphasizes the contextual fluidity of his language in ways strikingly similar to the work of Gayatri Spivak and others in postcolonialism and deconstruction. The opening essay in *Bulletproof Buddhists* once again highlights Chin's longstanding commitments to the disruption of, rather than opposition to, those narrative strategies and languages of race and ethnicity especially, that would aspire to contain him. Since youth, Chin recalls in "I Am Talking to the Strategist Sun Tzu," he has been a cipher within an American model of self-perception which is capable of rendering citizens, and their ethnic and gender makeup, only in discrete, identifiable ways. His response is not to counter such a system by asserting some alternate identity, but rather to exploit the "anti-Chinaman vision" he had critiqued in *Chickencoop*. Of his experiences taking multiple choice exams in high school, he realizes: "I know something they don't know and they want to get it out of me. I decide to keep it that way and graduate high school with a personality that doesn't show up on tests for one. I have the stealth personality" (6). Chin supplements this adolescent experience as he shuttles throughout the essay between a 1960 Fair Play for Cuba tour and a series of military analects that reinforce the lessons of stealth and survival: "*'The ultimate in disposing one's troops is to be without ascertainable shape. Then the most penetrating spies cannot pry in, nor can the wise lay plans against you'*" (17).

Thus, the opening essay in *Bulletproof* addresses any number of themes in Chin's work. He argues for the reclamation of actually existing history and culture of Chinese America as a relatively stable ground for the decidedly unstable stealth personality. However, he claims simultaneously that the reward of a renewed historical understanding of Chinaman experiences in America will be the ongoing redress of stereotyping and the fleeting, impermanent interruptions of the literary-cultural machines that replicate those stereotypes. Chin calls for diffuse rhetorical strategies, based in part on the "practical language skills of the here-and-now school" (68), that frustrate the dominant will to see Chinese cultural inheritance in America as something containable, something monolithic. In fact, Chin affirms the disruptive potential contained in Asian America's longstanding survival strategies, and in continually provoking—although never satisfying—the internal and external demands for identification: "Hungry, all the time hungry, every sense was out whiffing for something rightly ours, chameleons looking for color" (68).

The final essay in the collection finds Chin and his five-year-old son driving up Interstate 5 between Los Angeles and Seattle on a promotional tour for *Donald Duk*, and, continuing in the collection's provocative vein, "Pidgin Contest" addresses the continuation of racism in the 1990s under cover of a benign tolerance. The essay mourns the loss of anger from the landscape of popular culture. Illustrating the angry war of words that drives *Chickencoop* and seeks to disrupt structures of racism and racist language, Chin finds himself in downtown Portland, Oregon, surrounded by a new generation of adolescents who don't "know how to cuss" (416). As he reflects on the encounter Chin continues: "I see this need to teach our young how to properly cuss and offend with the specificity of a smart bomb as the first step toward full literacy and I-5 civility. You read to get the knowledge you need to win a fight, or, in this case, pick a fight, and avoid a fight" (417). Chin continues to employ the voice of his longstanding public persona of anger and confrontation against dominant American culture; yet, keeping in the vein of the Sun Tzu analects that opened the collection, Chin deploys anger strategically as a mediating force, through which his readers acknowledge their prejudices and constantly engage in the reinvention of languages of civility. Turning the early 1990s buzzword of "political correctness" on its head, Chin writes:

> I suggest PC stand for *pidgin contest*.
> Civil language and tolerant behavior can't be imposed from the top without exercising heavy police-state censorship and driving everyone with a discouraging word underground. But in the bustling, competitive, passionate marketplace atmosphere of a port city or corner store, civil language and tolerant behavior are invented, or you go broke, brah. (418)

Indeed, the longstanding critical disdain for Chin's language games—especially for his refusal to comply with top-down demands for tolerance—is trumped in this critique. However, for Chin, the ethnic separation following the dismissal of charges against police who beat Rodney King created a "vision of LA beyond *Bladerunner*, and not real [. . .]. It's all grotesque exaggeration. And it's impossible to choose up sides" (423).

Chin's conclusion speaks to the irresolvable tensions that inhabit not only Asian American literature specifically, but also American literature and culture generally, all of which are impermanent material and ideal spaces that are constantly being created and devastated, lauded and dismissed. Chin's always provocative ability to illustrate these literary and cultural tensions plays a key role in the small body of critical work that addresses his writing; in addition to David Leiwei Li, Jinqi Ling and I have attempted to trace Chin's complex treatment of numerous cultural, literary, and historical phenomena. Most significantly, the goal of this recent work has not been either the support of or the reversal of the longstanding totalizing claims about Chin or his corpus; rather, it strives to bring to light the significance of the irresolvable questions and problems that Chin has been posing to his readers for more than three decades.

CHIN AS LITERARY HISTORIAN

The angry critical voice that emerges in Chin's fiction and in his treatments of Asian American literature and culture arises largely from his experiences of the 1960s as an aspiring writer. Faced with the ostensible absence of literary works by Asian Americans, Chin began to wonder whether he was the first to produce Asian American fiction that was not caught up in generic constraints of the cookbook and the autobiography, forms that, for Chin, represented the longstanding bind between racist love and racist hate in which Asian American histories and cultures were caught. The "Chinese American publishing sensations" who emerged into the

American literary consciousness in the late nineteenth and early twentieth centuries apparently internalized this dynamic and appealed to broad stereotypes of Asians as "subcutaneous white supremacists" ("Come" 8, 9). Books such as Pardee Lowe's *Father and Glorious Descendent* (1943) and Jade Snow Wong's *Fifth Chinese Daughter* (1953) succeeded by "mak[ing] art of the stereotype" and served as the avatars of "legitimate" Asian American literature by providing the narrative forms and representational strategies for successive generations ("Come" 8). Forging a contrary path, Chin sought out and publicized an alternate literary history that would strongly influence the development of an undercurrent of Asian American writing in the 1970s.

In 1974, Chin, along with Shawn Wong, Lawson Inada, and Jeffery Paul Chan, published a collection of modern and early contemporary works by Chinese American and Japanese American writers. *Aiiieeeee! An Anthology of Asian American Writers* (1974) presented "fifty years of our whole voice" (Chan xi); the volume would serve as the evidence of an Asian American literary tradition that was not influenced solely by autobiographical forms and themes. In order to unearth a literary history other than the partial, culturally skewed archive of autobiographies and testimonial narratives that were popularly available, the Aiiieeeee! group recalls having to overcome their own processes of forgetting the literary-cultural histories by which they had been surrounded throughout their lives. "Way past our childhoods," they write in the introduction to *The Big Aiiieeeee!*,

> we had to gather "the stuff of the real" the hard way. We had to ask, inspect, corroborate, challenge, and prove the factual, textual reality of the stuff and its place in Asian universal knowledge. As we suspected, contrary to the stereotype, Chinese and Japanese immigrants were a literate people from literate civilizations whose presses, theaters,

opera houses, and artistic enterprises rose as quickly as their social and political institutions. They are not few. They are not gone. They are not stupid. They were only waiting to be asked. (xv-xvi)

Although they focus largely on Chinese American and Japanese American literary histories, the two *Aiiieeeee!* collections remain vital resources for students of Asian American literature. As Filipina American author Jessica Hagedorn recalls in the introduction to her own anthology, *Charlie Chan Is Dead* (1993): "Receiving my copy [of *Aiiieeeee!*] as a gift from Frank Chin [. . .] proved a joyous revelation. I was not alone, pure and simple. [. . .] The energy and interest sparked by *Aiiieeeee!* in the seventies was essential to Asian American writers because it gave us visibility and credibility as creators of our own specific literature. We could not be ignored" (xxvi-xxvii). The Aiiieeeee! group would later receive much criticism for the limits they had placed on the works and/or authors they included and excluded from the collection; nonetheless, their opening salvo in the battle for reclamation and continuing development of Asian American literary voices was a voice of confrontation against an otherwise monolithic literary landscape.

In addition to the two anthologies, one of the most significant endeavors in Chin's longstanding commitment to the reclamation of Asian American literary history is found in his republishing of John Okada's novel, *No-No Boy*. In 1970 Jeffery Chan and the Aiiieeeee! group rediscovered the forgotten novel, which, in the midst of the Red Scare and other injunctions to hyperpatriotism following World War Two, had failed to sell even its first printing; they subsequently formed the Combined Asian Resources Project (CARP) in order to republish the novel. As Chin recalls, the CARP edition quickly sold out its initial printings, largely to a readership of Japanese Americans "who were ready to look back at themselves" after years of attempting—at least in public discourse—to believe the assimilationist fictions proffered by leading Japanese American figures. Additionally, as he continues in his Afterword, "In Search of John Okada" (1976), "*No-No Boy* proved I wasn't the only yellow writer in yellow history. The book was so good it freed me to be trivial. [. . .] John Okada shows the 'identity' crisis to be both totally real and absolutely fake in a book that is still too strong for many yellows to read" (254-55). Thus, the significance of *No-No Boy* exceeds the novel itself, for it speaks to the entire history of reception of Asian American literature, and especially to the early contemporary writers of the Aiiieeeee! group who would follow Okada both in the sensibilities they brought to their work and in their critical reception.

By the time Chin and friends traced Okada, he had died, and his wife had burned all of his papers, including the first draft of a novel about Issei experience. Chin recalls his 1971 meeting with Dorothy Okada:

> After John died she offered all of John's manuscripts, notes and correspondence to the Japanese American Research Project at UCLA. John Okada was then and is now [in 1976] the only known Japanese American novelist. His *No-No Boy*, the only Japanese American novel. He belongs to Japanese American history and American literature, but the Japanese American Research Project refused to so much as look at the Okada papers. These champions of Japanese American history encouraged Dorothy to destroy the papers. (257)

The established repository for all things legitimately Japanese American rejected not only Okada's novel and written corpus, but also the author himself, whom Chin would later call the "only great one" of Seattle's Japanese American writers (260). For Chin, then, *No-No Boy* serves as the index for a broader history of reception of Asian American literature, which appears as an endlessly repeating cycle of literary innovations and experimentations that are soon overshadowed by works that appeal to dominant sensibilities alone. Those sensibilities in turn determine the economic future of favored works through sales, and, furthermore, determine the cultural capital that accrues to them through canonization. Through his discovery of Okada's forgotten novel, Chin revises his self-perception and the role of his writing, because he no longer feels called upon to be the sole innovator and occupant of literary Asian American fiction. Although the belated discovery of Okada provides Chin with a forebear, his consequent freedom "to be trivial" also threatens to leave Chin's own literary assays—at least during his lifetime—off the radar of a broad readership until the next generation discovers and, retroactively, assesses their significance.

Chin's latest work is another step in his reconstruction of the various Asian American literary histories that have been lost or marginalized, especially since World War Two. Additionally, *USA ni umarete—Born in the USA* (2002) provocatively sounds the themes of Okada's missing second novel. As Chin explains, it is a critical cultural study that formally cites John Dos Passos' *USA Trilogy* (1937) by reclaiming the historical complexity of "the Japanese American response to Pearl Harbor, and the fracturing of the community into contending groups that followed." Chin's point of departure is, as it was in "Come All Ye Asian American Writers," the tense relationship between competing histories of ethnic Asians in the United States. Most significantly, the Japanese American histories treated in *USA ni umarete* are, like their Chinese American counterparts, shot through in varying degrees by the fantasies and myths, as well as the political and cultural desires, of multiple generations of both dominant and marginal groups. "The Issei," Chin writes in his preface, "set up newspapers, hotels, Japanese American and Chinese restaurants and entertainment halls while the whites applied pressure in popular song and novels to deny the Japanese Americans their civil rights, and the right to own or lease land. The Nisei grew up on these songs and novels." Chin then proceeds through these contested narrative and historical spaces, incorporating materials from popular songs, magazine and newspaper articles, diaries and testimonies, not to totalize the legacy of internment, but rather to pursue its surprising complexity against the grain of popular conception.

CONCLUSION

Chin's resistance to creating a stable narrative of, or for, a century of ethnic Japanese experiences in America indicates that he continues to perceive Asian American literature and history through a hybrid, conflictual multiplicity of texts, oral histories, and past and present experiences, rather than through a single explanatory narrative. On the other hand, as Chin scans the current scene of culturally and/or academically sanctioned Asian American literary studies, he finds that the field remains committed to relatively stable, monolithic concerns. He claims,

> The teaching of Asian American Literature follows religious, not objective rules. Instructors don't feel embarrassed about announcing that I am banned in their classes. [. . .] Asian American lit. will not be taken seriously as long as the rules guiding its teaching are whimsical and the teachers follow their stupidity instead of their knowledge. (Chin, Personal Interview)

Still contentious, Chin remains an unapologetically activist author and public figure, and, like many activists, his longstanding commitments may be recognized only belatedly, if at all.

It is on those terms of belated recognition that I close by returning once again to the prescience of *Year of the Dragon*'s Fred Eng, who spoke some three decades ago to the fate of the activist artist who is caught between the desire for legitimacy and the impossibility of its attainment:

> I don't wanta be a pioneer. Just a writer. Just see my name in a book by me. About things I like writing about, and fuck the pioneers. What've the old pioneers done for us, for me? I'm not even fighting nobody. I just have a few words and they come at me. "Be Chinese, Charlie Chan, or a nobody" to the whites and a mad dog to the Chinamans . . . for what? To die and be discovered by some punk in the next generation and published in mimeograph by some college ethnic studies department, forget it. (117)

Through Fred, Chin presented a critique of the space that he would, nonetheless, come to claim for himself through his literary and critical production. A generation after the staging of *Year of the Dragon*, as Fred forecasts, the fictional component of Chin's own corpus is being read more frequently, even despite the fact that much of that work has slipped out of print. Indeed, the burden for rediscovery and reactivation will likely fall on the students, not the teachers who, as Chin suggests, will remain trapped by the lures of doctrinal and disciplinary stability. Furthermore, those students will be the first to break from the longstanding injunction to disregard not only Chin, but also the broad range of Asian American literatures that have threatened to rupture the limits established by a body of safe and sanctioned works.

I think, too, that the current gestures toward reassessing both the critical and fictional components of Chin's work are more than efforts to recuperate the reputation of a single author alone. As Chin has served a stable function in the field of Asian American literature as its negative index, new consideration of his work will also draw students toward a renewed consideration of the field at large, and for the role of Asian American literary and cultural studies in the broader domain of contemporary American literature. Chin's work would threaten, in fact, to dismantle the perceived permanence of such literary and critical categories as he interrogates them with dialogic forms "as formal or as formless as you chose" ("This" 112). Keeping the themes of transience at work throughout his corpus, Chin continues to think of the historical, cultural, linguistic, and literary identities of Asian Americans as contested processes rather than as permanently given totalities. In the face of the institutional ignorance of Chin, and the perceived responsibility to dismiss his work as a totality, we find the best evidence of what Chin has called a waning of the will to fight, to provoke constantly the boundaries of tolerance, good taste, and the like. As Chin writes, in fact, there must be a responsibility for discussion—or in his favored term, dialogue—that constantly pushes at, disrupts, and only tacitly reformulates Asian American literature, identity, and culture.

Selected Bibliography

Amirthanayagam, Guy, ed. *Asian and Western Writers in Dialogue.* London: Macmillan, 1982.
Chan, Jeffery Paul, et al., eds. *Aiiieeeee!: An Anthology of Asian-American Writers.* Washington, D.C.: Howard UP, 1974.
——. *The Big Aiiieeeee!.* New York: Meridian, 1991.
Chan, Jeffery, and Marilyn C. Alquiloza. "Asian-American Literary Traditions." *A Literary History of the American West.* Fort Worth: Texas Christian UP, 1987. 1119-38.
Cheung, King-Kok. *Articulate Silences.* Ithaca: Cornell UP, 1993.
——. "Re-viewing Asian American Literary Studies." Cheung, ed., *An Interethnic Guide*, 1-36.
——, ed. *An Interethnic Guide to Asian American Literature.* New York: Cambridge, 1997.
Chin, Frank. "Afterward." *MELUS* 3.2 (1976): 13-17.
——. *Bulletproof Buddhists.* Honolulu: U of Hawaii P, 1998.
——. *The Chickencoop Chinaman and The Year of the Dragon: Two Plays by Frank Chin.* Seattle: U of Washington P, 1981.
——. *The Chinaman Pacific & Frisco R.R. Co.* Minneapolis: Coffee House, 1988.
——. "Come All Ye Asian American Writers of the Real and the Fake." *The Big Aiiieeeee!* Ed. Jeffery Paul Chan, et al. New York: Meridian, 1991. 1-92.
——. *Donald Duk.* Minneapolis: Coffee House, 1991.
——. *Gunga Din Highway.* Minneapolis: Coffee House, 1994.
——. "In Search of John Okada." Okada, 253-60.
——. Personal Interview with John Charles Goshert. 30 Mar. 2002.

———. "Racist Love." *Seeing Through Shuck.* Ed. Richard Kostelanetz. New York: Ballantine, 1972. 65-79.

———. "Rashomon Road." *Multi-America.* Ed. Ishmael Reed. New York: Penguin, 1998. 286-308.

———. "This is Not an Autobiography." *Genre* 18 (1985): 109-30.

———. *USA ni umarete—Born in the USA.* Lanham, MD: Rowman and Littlefield, 2002.

Chu, Patricia. "Tripmaster Monkey, Frank Chin, and the Chinese Heroic Tradition." *Arizona Quarterly* 53.3 (1997): 117-39.

Davis, Robert Murray. "Introduction." *Genre* 18 (1985): 105-08.

Ghymn, Esther Milyung. *Images of Asian American Women by Asian American Writers.* New York: Lang, 1995.

Gish, Robert F. "Reperceiving Ethnicity in Western American Literature." *Updating the Literary West.* Fort Worth: Texas Christian UP, 1997. 35-43.

Goshert, John. "'Frank Chin Is Not a Part of this Class!': Thinking at the Limits of Asian American Literature." *Jouvert* 4.3 (2000): unpaginated article (39 paragraphs). <http://social.chass.ncsu.edu/jouvert/v4i3/Goshert.htm> (30 March 2002).

———. "A Minor Incision: Transdisciplinarity and the Discourses of Marginality." *Janus Head* (Winter 2001): 159-77.

Goudie, S.X. "Theory, Practice, and the Intellectual: A Conversation with Abdul R. JanMohamed." *Jouvert* 1.2 (1997): unpaginated article. <http://social.chass.ncsu.edu/jouvert/v1i2/Goudie.htm> (30 March 2002).

Guillory, John. *Cultural Capital.* Chicago: U of Chicago P, 1993.

Hagedorn, Jessica, ed. *Charlie Chan is Dead.* New York: Penguin, 1993.

Haslam, Gerald. "Introduction." *A Literary History of the American West.* Fort Worth: Texas Christian UP, 1987. 1017-25.

JanMohamed, Abdul R., and David Lloyd. "Introduction: Toward a Theory of Minority Discourse: What is to be Done?" JanMohamed and Lloyd, eds., 1-16.

—, eds. *The Nature and Context of Minority Discourse*. Oxford: Oxford UP, 1990.

Kim, Elaine H. "Defining Asian American Realities Through Literature." JanMohamed and Lloyd, eds., 146-70.

—. "Such Opposite Creatures: Men and Women in Asian American Literature." *Michigan Quarterly* 29 (1990): 68-93.

Kingston, Maxine Hong. "Cultural Mis-readings by American Reviewers." Amirthanayagam, ed., 55-65.

—. "Violence and Non-Violence in China, 1989." *Michigan Quarterly* 29 (1990): 62-67.

Lee, Rachel. *The Americas of Asian American Literature*. Princeton: Princeton UP, 1999.

Li, David Leiwei. "The Formation of Frank Chin and Formations of Chinese American Literature." *Asian Americans: Comparative and Global Perspectives*. Ed. Shirley Hune, et al. Pullman: Washington State UP, 1991. 211-23.

—. *Imagining the Nation: Asian American Literature and Cultural Consent*. Stanford: Stanford UP, 1993.

—. "The Production of Chinese American Tradition: Displacing American Orientalist Discourse." Lim and Ling, eds., 319-31.

Lim, Shirley Geok-Lin, and Amy Ling, eds. *Reading the Literatures of Asian America*. Philadelphia: Temple UP, 1992.

Ling, Jinqi. "Identity Crisis and Gender Politics: Reappropriating Asian American Masculinity." Cheung, ed.. *An Interethnic Guide*, 312-37.

Liu, Toming Jun. "The Problematics of Kingston's 'Cultural Translation': A Chinese Diasporic View of *The Woman Warrior*." *Journal of American Studies of Turkey* 4 (1996): 15-30.

Lowe, John. "Monkey Kings and Mojo: Postmodern Ethnic Humor in Kingston, Reed, and Vizenor." *MELUS* 21.4 (1996): 103-26.

McDonald, Dorothy Ritsuko. "Introduction." Chin, The Chickencoop, ix-xxix.

Okada, John. *No-No Boy*. 1957. Seattle: U of Washington P, 1986.

Palumbo-Liu, David. "Introduction." *The Ethnic Canon*. Ed. David Palumbo-Liu. Minneapolis: U of Minnesota P, 1995. 1-27.

Radhakrishnan, R. "Ethnic Identity and Post-Structuralist Difference." JanMohamed and Lloyd, eds., 50-71.

Reed, Ishmael, ed. *19 Necromancers from Now*. Garden City, NY: Doubleday, 1970.

——. *Multi-America*. New York: Penguin, 1998.

Simon, Myron. "Two Angry Ethnic Writers." *MELUS* 3.2 (1976): 20-24.

Skenazy, Paul, and Tera Martin, eds. *Conversations With Maxine Hong Kingston*. Jackson: UP of Mississippi, 1998.

Vizenor, Gerald. "Ethnic Derivatives: Tricksterese versus Anthropologetics." Reed, *Multi-America*, 373-80.

Wong, Sau-Ling Cynthia. "'Sugar Sisterhood': Situating the Amy Tan Phenomenon." Palumbo-Liu, ed., 174-210.

Wong, Shawn, ed. *Asian American Literature*. New York: Longman, 1996.